DON'T PANIC IT'S PUBERTY!

A Guide for Girls

Anna Claybourne &
Jennifer Naalchigar

FRANKLIN WATTS
LONDON • SYDNEY

First published in Great Britain in 2023 by Hodder & Stoughton

Copyright © Hodder & Stoughton Limited, 2023

All rights reserved.

Credits
Series Editor: Julia Bird
Series Designer: Lisa Peacock
Consultant: Dr Kristina Routh
Illustrations: Jennifer Naalchigar

HB ISBN: 978 1 4451 8648 1
PB ISBN: 978 1 4451 8647 4

Printed in the UK

London Borough of Enfield	
91200000811335	
Askews & Holts	24-Apr-2024
J612.661 JUNIOR NON-	
ENWINC	

Franklin Watts
An imprint of
Hachette Children's Group
Part of Hodder & Stoughton
Carmelite House
50 Victoria Embankment
London EC4Y 0DZ

An Hachette UK Company
www.hachette.co.uk
www.hachettechildrens.co.uk

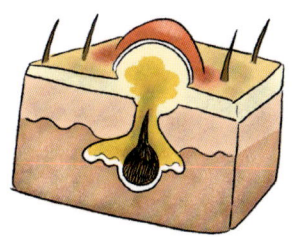
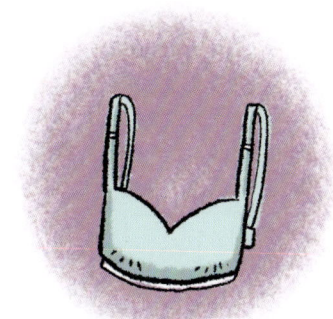

Contents

- 4 Don't panic!
- 6 All about your body – on the outside
- 8 All about your body – on the inside
- 10 Hello hormones!
- 12 I'm growing!
- 14 I'm growing BOOBS!
- 16 Periods – WHY?
- 18 Periods – sorted!
- 20 The skin you're in
- 22 What's that hair doing there?
- 24 Eating and exercise
- 26 Zzzzzzzzzz.....
- 28 Puberty for your brain
- 30 In a mood!
- 32 Feeling OK – or not OK?
- 34 Strange new feelings
- 36 Friends and fitting in
- 38 Say no to sexism!
- 40 When does it end?
- 42 Puberty timeline
- 44 Frequently asked questions
- 46 Glossary & further reading
- 48 Index

DON'T PANIC!

Sometime between the ages of about 8 and 13, you start to go through a big change, called puberty. It lasts for a few years, and during that time, you change from a child into an adult.

CHANGES EVERYWHERE!

Puberty is not really just one big change. It's made up of lots of changes, and they can happen in different ways and at different times.

There are changes you can see ...

... like your body changing shape ...

... and suddenly getting taller!

And there are also changes in your brain, mind and feelings.

Oooh, look how much you've grown!

There are changes inside your body too ... such as starting to have periods! (What are they? See pages 16-19!)

WHY IS IT CALLED THAT?
Puberty is a strange word, but its meaning is simple. It comes from an old Latin word, pubertas, meaning 'grown up'.

HOW DO YOU FEEL?

It's normal to have different feelings about going through puberty – including fears, worries and even feeling angry or upset.

But there's a plus side, too. Yes, really! Sometimes, you might feel really happy and excited about growing up.

It's your pathway to being an adult, when you can have more freedom and fun, make your own decisions, do what YOU want to do, and rule your own life!

ALL YOU NEED TO KNOW

This book is your no-panic guide to puberty, and all the changes it brings.
Inside you'll discover:
- How your body works, and what's going on inside it.
- What to expect during puberty, and how to handle it.
- And answers to lots of questions you might have.

Let's get started!

ALL ABOUT YOUR BODY – ON THE OUTSIDE

Puberty begins with your body. The reason it happens is to help you change from a child into an adult, who can have children. (Of course, you might not want to do that, and you don't have to – but the changes happen anyway!)

YOU'RE AN ANIMAL!
Why does it work like this? Well, humans are a type of animal.

Just like all animals, we have a life cycle. We're born, we get bigger, and then we become adults who can have babies and carry on the cycle.

Pregnancy

Baby

Child

Puberty

Adult

Puberty is the change that makes this possible. It's a bit like when a caterpillar changes into a butterfly!

TIME FOR A CHANGE
So let's take a look at the female body, and the things that change during puberty.

Your skin can get more oily, which can cause spots.

Armpits start growing tufty hair, and get more sweaty.

You grow breasts (also called boobs).

Your body becomes slightly curvier all over.

Your hips grow wider.

You grow taller, sometimes 'shooting up' quickly.

Hair called pubic hair grows here. It's often curly, even if the hair on your head is straight!

WHAT'S HAPPENING TO ME?!
When your body first starts changing, it can feel really weird. You have to get used to a new body shape and whole new body parts. Clothes might fit differently, and some girls feel self-conscious about other people noticing the changes.

ALL ABOUT YOUR BODY – ON THE INSIDE

It's not just how your body looks on the outside that's changing. There are all kinds of things going on inside, too ...

BABY-MAKING BITS

Inside their bodies, girls have a set of body parts called the reproductive system. These are the parts that allow women to get pregnant and have a baby. During puberty, these parts grow bigger, and gradually start working.

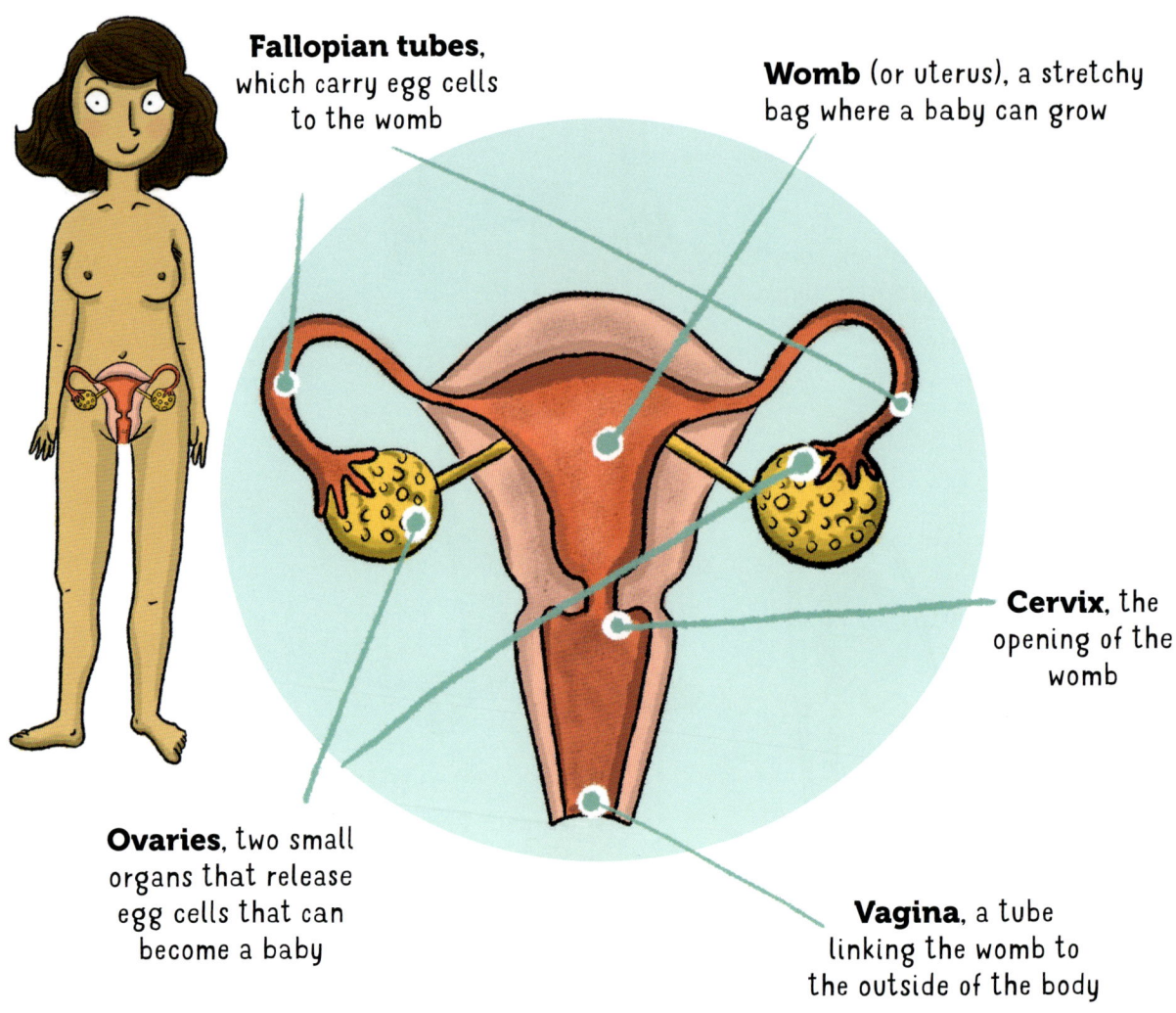

Fallopian tubes, which carry egg cells to the womb

Womb (or uterus), a stretchy bag where a baby can grow

Cervix, the opening of the womb

Ovaries, two small organs that release egg cells that can become a baby

Vagina, a tube linking the womb to the outside of the body

8

WHICH IS WHICH?

A lot of people (even some adults!) get confused about what the vagina is. So let's clear that up right now! The **vagina** is inside the body. It's a tube leading from a hole between your legs, up to the womb. The parts around the entrance to the vagina have a different name. Together, they're called the **vulva**, or sometimes the **genitals**.

VULVA VIEW

Because of where it is, it can be pretty hard to see your vulva! But it's useful to know what's there.

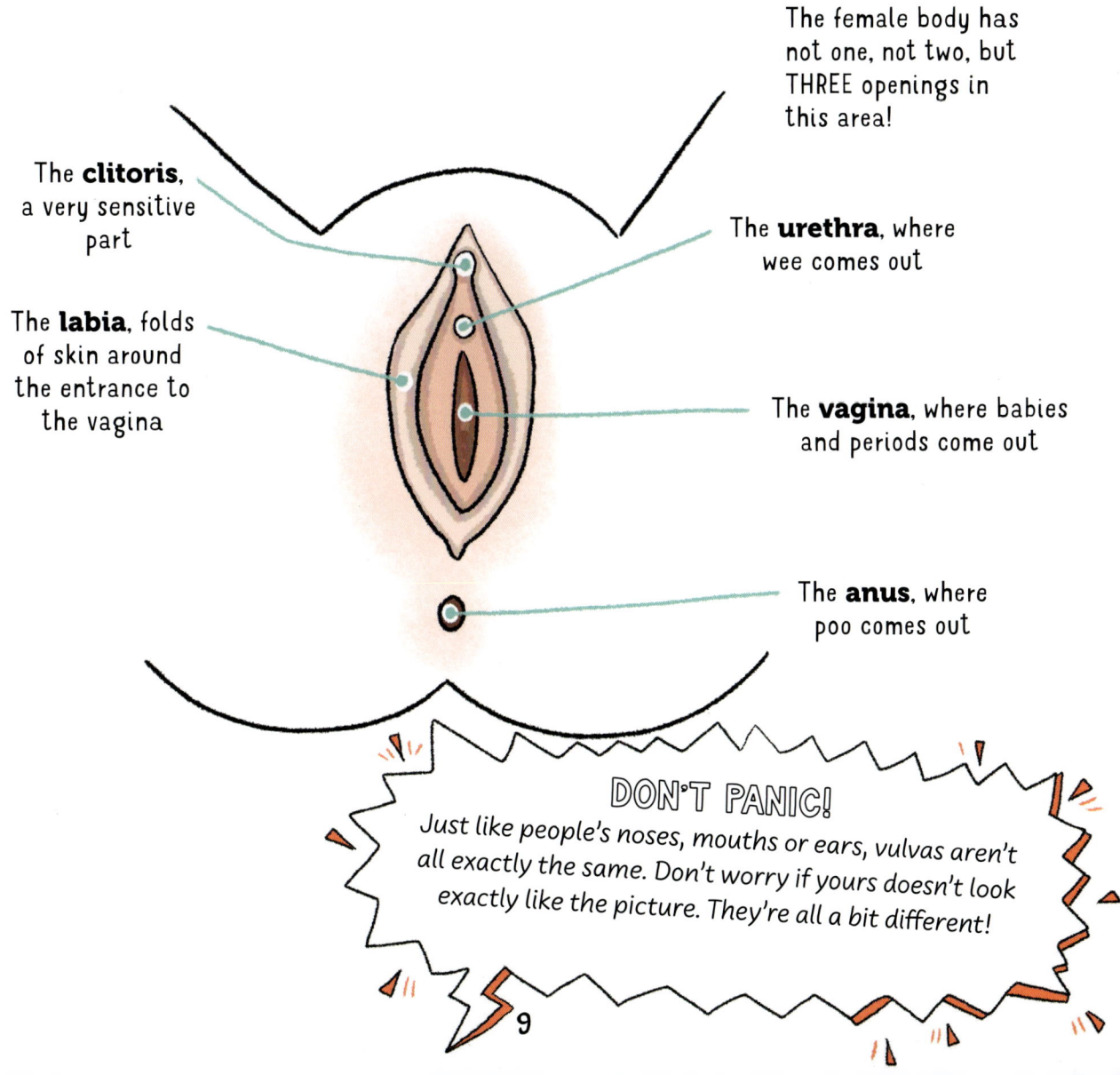

The female body has not one, not two, but THREE openings in this area!

The **clitoris**, a very sensitive part

The **labia**, folds of skin around the entrance to the vagina

The **urethra**, where wee comes out

The **vagina**, where babies and periods come out

The **anus**, where poo comes out

DON'T PANIC!

Just like people's noses, mouths or ears, vulvas aren't all exactly the same. Don't worry if yours doesn't look exactly like the picture. They're all a bit different!

HELLO HORMONES!

So how does your body know when to start changing, and how? The answer is **hormones!** Hormones are chemicals that send messages around the body, telling it what to do.

HANDY HORMONES
Hormones don't just control puberty. They have lots of other jobs too.

* When you're scared, the hormone **adrenaline** makes your heart beat faster, in case you need to run away.

* The hormone **insulin** is released when you eat. It helps your body to turn food into energy.

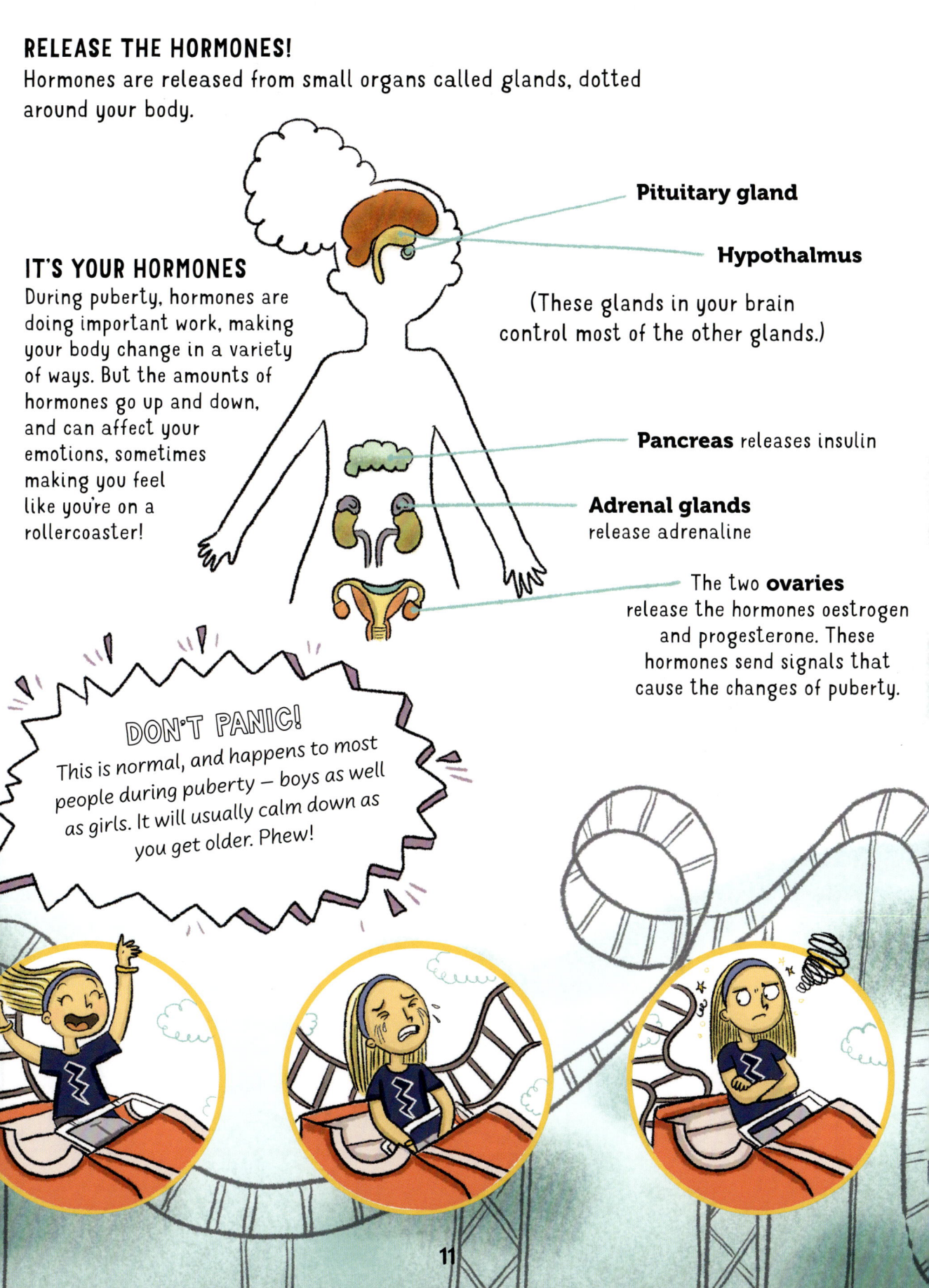

I'M GROWING!

During puberty, you can expect to grow to your adult height. Depending on how tall you end up, that could be a LOT of growing ...

HOW TALL WILL I BE?

The average height of an adult woman is about 160 cm, or 5 feet 3 inches. However, height varies a lot, and it depends on many things - especially your genes. Genes are parts found inside your cells, passed on to you from your parents, that help to control your body shape.

SO IF PEOPLE IN YOUR FAMILY ARE TALLER THAN AVERAGE, YOU COULD WELL BE TOO!

DON'T PANIC! Growing fast can mean you get aches and pains. See a doctor if you're worried, but there's usually no need to panic.

WHEN WILL I GET THERE?

It varies, but most girls reach their adult height by about 15. You'll probably find you sometimes grow slowly, and sometimes have a 'growth spurt' when you grow really fast!

FAST FEET
Your feet can have growth spurts too! Annoying if you've just got new shoes...

I'M TOO TALL! I'M TOO SHORT!

No you're not! Lots of girls (and boys too) worry about their height, and wish they were taller or shorter. But humans come in a wide range of normal, healthy heights and body shapes. Being extra-tall or short might be annoying in some ways – but useful in others!

You can always see the band!

You can always find shoes that fit!

I'M GROWING BOOBS!

Breasts, or boobs, are often one of the first signs of puberty to appear. And they're often something girls panic about, too!

IT STARTS WITH A BUMP ...
Breasts usually start forming between the ages of 8 and 11 – sometimes even earlier.

The first sign is a small bump under each nipple, called a **breast bud**. They can sometimes feel a bit sore.

Gradually, the breasts grow into a rounder shape.

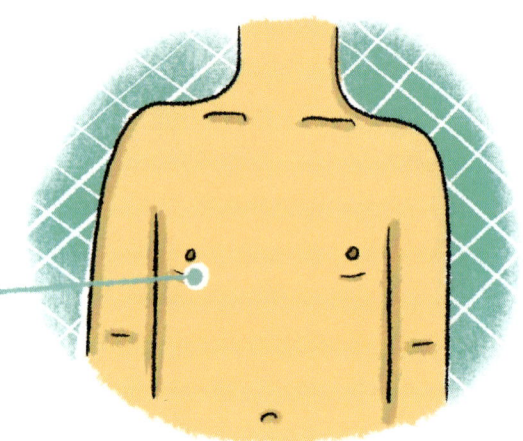

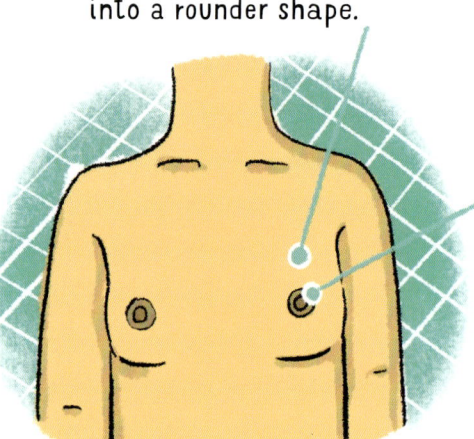

This part around the nipple, called the **areola**, gets bigger.

The nipples can get darker too, but this doesn't always happen.

Breasts often keep growing all the way through puberty.

They usually reach their full size by about age 16 or 17.

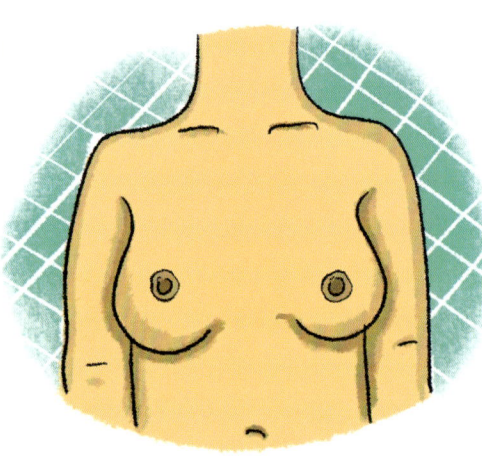

WHAT ARE THEY FOR?
After a woman gives birth to a baby, her breasts make milk, which she can use to feed the baby.

TIME FOR A BRA?

Bras surround your boobs, supporting them and making them feel more comfortable. When you feel like wearing a bra might be a good idea, you could ask your mum, or someone like a big sister or auntie, to help you choose some.

Soft, stretchy bras like this are ideal for boobs that are still growing.

Crop top style

Spaghetti straps

Racerback

DON'T PANIC!
Breasts come in many different shapes and sizes, so don't worry if yours don't look exactly like your friends'. Sometimes, one boob is a bit bigger than the other — don't panic, it's normal! They usually even out a bit as you get older.

Some bras have thin foam pads inside to give boobs a bit more protection.

PERIODS – WHY?

When you first hear about periods, you might think: WHAT?! WHY?
And that's a very good question!

WHAT IS A PERIOD?
When you have a period, it means some blood comes out of your vagina. It lasts for a few days, and happens roughly once a month.

That might sound a bit scary, because normally, if you're bleeding, it means you're hurt. But don't panic! Periods are totally normal. They are a sign that it is possible for you to have a baby.

REALLY?!!

WHEN DO PERIODS START?
Periods usually start around the age of 12, but it's sometimes earlier or later. At first, they can be light, with very little blood. They might also take a while to settle down into a regular cycle.

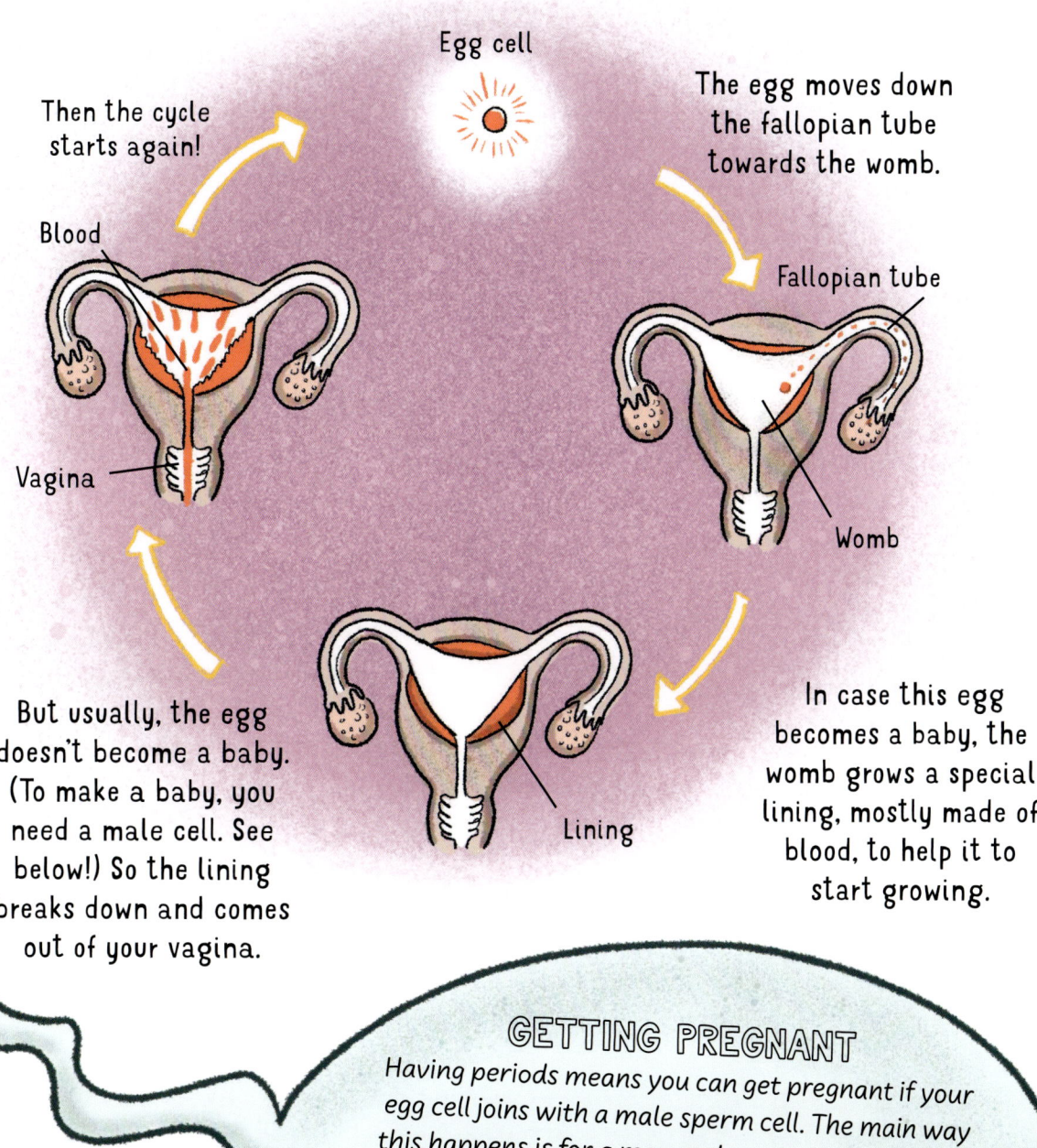

PERIODS – SORTED!

Period blood leaks out in drips and drops over a few days. So you need a way to catch it!

Luckily, there are lots of ways to do this, and products to help you, called period products or sanitary products. You can find them in supermarkets and chemists, or buy them online. Sometimes, you can get them free from your school, or a library or health centre.

SANITARY PAD
These soft, absorbent pads fit inside your pants and soak up the blood. They come in different sizes and thicknesses.

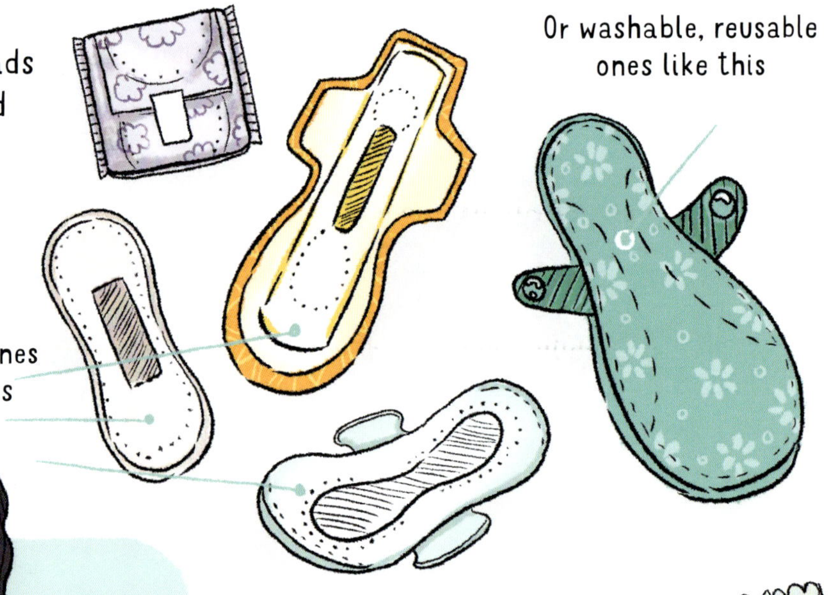

Or washable, reusable ones like this

You can get disposable ones that stick to your pants

PERIOD PANTS
These look like normal pants, but have a pad built in. You throw them in the washing machine just like other undies! They're more expensive than normal pants, but save money on other period products.

TAMPONS

A tampon is a little cylinder that fits inside the vagina and soaks up the blood. It has a string so you can easily pull it out again.

Tampon

Some tampons have an applicator (used to put the tampon in)

Tampons can be useful. But some girls find them uncomfortable or difficult to put in, so pads or pants can be easier to start with.

HOW MUCH BLOOD?

Not that much! It's usually only about 2-4 tablespoons, or 30-60ml, over 3-5 days.

That's about this much.

DOES IT HURT?

It doesn't hurt when the blood comes out, but some girls get a dull, aching pain in the womb area. Normal painkillers and a hot water bottle can help. (But check with a trusted adult before taking any painkillers.)

DON'T PANIC!
Instead, BE PREPARED! It's a good idea to have a little emergency pack of pads and spare pants in your bag. You can also keep track of your cycle, to help you predict your next period. (Though it might not always stick to the plan!)

THE SKIN YOU'RE IN

Puberty can affect your skin too, in several different ways. And some of them can be very annoying!

SWEATY SKIN

Everyone sweats, especially when they're hot. However, when puberty strikes, you might find you get a bit more sweaty than you used to. Sweat can start to smell stronger too, especially in particular areas.

It's not a problem though, as long as you keep clean. Have a quick shower or wash every day, or after doing sport or exercise. You might also want to start using a deodorant.

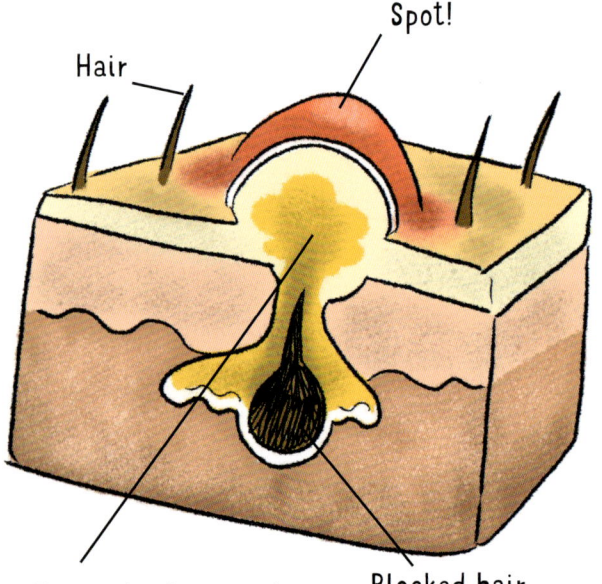

ZAP THE ZITS!

Spots, also called zits, pimples or acne, are little bumps on your skin. Puberty hormones can make your skin produce extra oil, or sebum. It can get trapped in the tiny hair follicles in your skin, along with bacteria. This creates a swelling that can become red and painful.

TO DEAL WITH SPOTS:
- Keep your skin clean, and wash your face well every morning and evening.
- Try not to squeeze, poke or pick at spots – it can make them worse!
- Anti-spot cream, gel or facewash might help – ask your pharmacist for advice.
- You can also use concealer make-up to cover spots, if you like.

DON'T PANIC!
You might be lucky – not everyone gets spots. Or you might only get a few. But if spots are really getting you down, see a doctor about them, as they should be able to help.

STRE-EE-ETCH!
If you grow very quickly during puberty, you can get stretch marks. The skin on your back, hips, stomach or legs actually gets stretched, leaving stripy-looking marks. But don't panic – they fade after a while!

From this ...   ... to this.

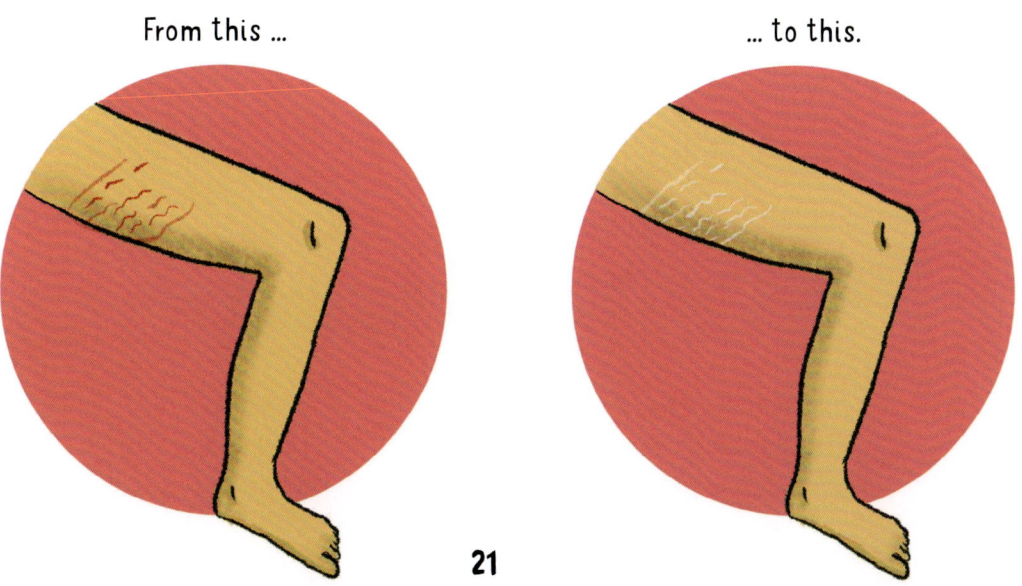

WHAT'S THAT HAIR DOING THERE?

Some time after puberty starts, you start growing hair in places you didn't have hair before!

It can vary from one person to another, but most girls will find ...

You grow little tufts of hair in your armpits.

Some girls get fine hair on their upper lip.

Pubic hair grows above and around the vulva.

The hair on your arms and legs can get thicker or darker.

You won't grow all this hair at once. It usually starts to appear gradually, from the age of around 9 or 10, then gets thicker over the next few years.

WHAT'S IT FOR?

Body hair has lots of uses. It carries sweat away from the skin, and protects sensitive areas like the vulva. It can even help to keep germs away from your skin.

REMOVING HAIR

Despite this, both women and men have been removing body hair for centuries. Men have been shaving the hair off their faces since ancient times, for example.

LOOKING GOOD!

DON'T PANIC!

Fashions for removing hair come and go, and are different in different cultures. But in the end, it's up to YOU what you do with your own body — not anyone else. If you do decide you want to remove some body hair, talk it over with your mum or another female relative.

DON'T FORGET YOUR HEAD!

During puberty, you might find that the hair on your head gets more oily — especially if you also have oily skin. Don't panic — you just might need to wash it more often than you used to!

23

EATING AND EXERCISE

Puberty can be a pain, but there are simple everyday things that can make it easier – including eating healthy foods, and staying active.

FOOD, FABULOUS FOOD
You have to eat, but WHAT you eat can make a big difference to how you feel. Here's a handy guide to some healthy and helpful foods to try ...

• GROWING
You need plenty of protein to help you grow during puberty. It's found in meat and fish, but also in eggs, beans, tofu and nuts.

MORE GROWING ...
Vitamin D and calcium are important for growing strong bones. Milk, cheese and yoghurt, green leafy vegetables, mushrooms, salmon and eggs will help you to get more of these.

- Bun with seeds
- Beanburger
- Salad

... AND MORE GROWING!
Being in the sunshine helps your body make Vitamin D too, but make sure you wear plenty of sunscreen to protect your skin.

- **SKIN AND HAIR**
Healthy fats, found in olive oil, avocados, nuts and salmon, are great for keeping your skin and hair healthy. They're brilliant for your brain, too!

- **STRESS AND ANXIETY**
Did you know that some foods might be able to reduce stress and worry? Try a banana, dark chocolate or Brazil nuts.

GET MOVING!
Exercise is brilliant for helping you stay strong and healthy, and for reducing stress. If you're into sports, keep going! It will help you feel great, be social and stay healthy.

But if you don't like sport, that's OK. There are loads of other ways to get outdoors, get moving and feel good. How about …

Walking a dog
Dancing to your favourite songs
A day at the beach
Joining a parkrun
Dance or fitness classes — you could go with family or friends
Hiking, camping or climbing?

ZZZZZZZZZZZ......

As you get older you might be looking forward to staying up later at night – but during puberty, it's REALLY important to get enough sleep.

WHY DO WE NEED SLEEP?
Sleep is when your body rests, repairs injuries and builds new muscle and bone. It also keeps your immune system healthy, helping your body to fight germs and disease.

Sleep is vital for your brain too. It's when you store important memories and delete information you don't need.

Losing just one night of sleep can make you feel exhausted, confused and unwell.

BLERGHH...

That's why getting the sleep you need is one of the most important things you can do to make puberty easier!

HOW MUCH SLEEP?

Babies sleep almost all the time, but as you grow up you need less and less sleep. You still need quite a lot though! Check your age on the chart to see how much ...

8	10-10.5 hours
9	About 10 hours
10	9.5-10 hours
11	9-10 hours
12	9-9.5 hours
13	9-9.5 hours
14	About 9 hours
15	8-9 hours
16	8-9 hours

THESE AREN'T HELPING!

Unfortunately, some things can make it harder to get to sleep. Things like ...
- Looking at screens just before bed. Their bluish light puts your brain in 'awake' mode!
- Worrying about stuff.
- Having too much caffeine, found in coffee, tea and energy drinks.

To help you get a good night's sleep, try these:
- Be active during the day.
- Make sure your bedroom is dark, and not too hot.
- Avoid things containing caffeine.
- Switch off screens and devices at least one hour before bedtime.
- Try a warm bath, relaxing music or reading to help you wind down.

PUBERTY FOR YOUR BRAIN

While puberty is busy changing your body, there's fascinating stuff happening inside your brain too. Your brain doesn't just change and grow during puberty ... it actually gets REWIRED!

BRAIN TANGLE

Most of your brain is made up of a huge network of brain cells, connected together by long branches. When you think, understand or experience things, signals are zooming around the network. When you learn new things, they make new connections.

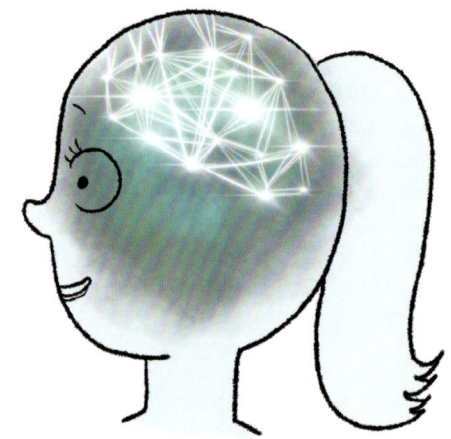

As you grow up, a series of changes happen in your brain.

NEWBORN
Newborn babies don't have many connections ...

AGE 6
... but they soon start taking in lots of information and building new connections. So small children have a lot!

AGE 14
As you get older, the brain deletes the connections you don't need, and makes the most useful ones stronger.

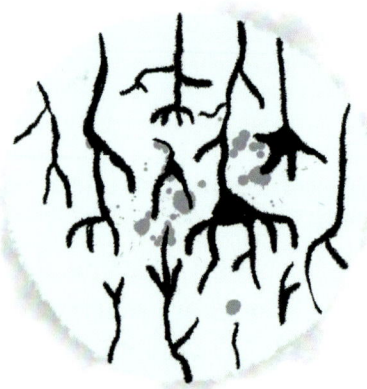
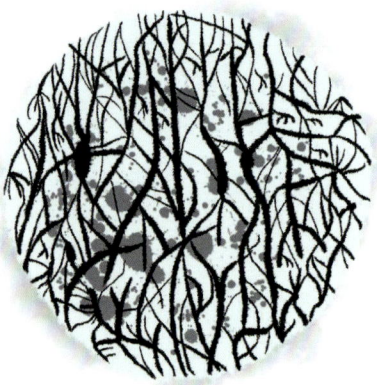

YOUR MATURING BRAIN
As this happens, your brain network gets more 'fixed', and you get slightly less good at learning new stuff. That's why small children pick up new words all the time, but learning a new language is harder when you're older.

THINK LIKE AN ADULT
However, the changes in your brain mean you DO get better at understanding things, seeing other people's point of view, and thinking decisions through. This takes a long time, though. Our brains aren't fully adult until around the age of 25!

OLD ENOUGH TO ...
Your maturing brain is why you're only allowed to do things like drive, vote or drink alcohol once you reach a certain age. As you get older, you're also more able to go out on your own and manage your money.

29

IN A MOOD!

With your hormones jumping around, your brain getting rewired, and your body springing all kinds of changes on you, it's no surprise that puberty can get a bit ... well ... STRESSFUL!

THIS WAY ... THAT WAY!
You might have a lot of 'mood swings' during puberty. Your mood can change quickly, and emotions can feel very strong. You might also have lots of different feelings at once.

This is all normal, and it will get easier as you get older. But it can still feel confusing, or even overwhelming.

PERIOD MOODS!
Once you start having periods, the hormones that control them can affect your moods, too. Many girls and women feel grumpy or irritable for a few days before their period.

STUFF TO DEAL WITH

During puberty, you often have to deal with other changes in your life. For example, you'll probably switch from primary to secondary school, which can be scary. Exams often happen during puberty, too. (Whose idea was THAT?)

DON'T PANIC!

You can't always solve all your problems, but you CAN learn ways to de-stress. Even little things can help you feel better. Here are some to try ...

- Cuddle or stroke a pet
- Listen to your favourite music
- Talk things over with a friend or relative
- Play a game, read a book or watch a funny TV show
- Get outdoors for a run or a walk with a friend.

FEELING OK – OR NOT OK?

Even if you have some mood swings and stressful times, you can get through them. And one thing that really helps with this is self-esteem.

WHAT IS IT?
Self-esteem means how you feel about yourself. If you have healthy self-esteem, it means you think you are OK! You accept and respect yourself.

If you have low self-esteem, it's harder to feel like this. You might blame yourself for your problems, or think you don't deserve help or support.

LOOK AFTER YOUR SELF-ESTEEM
Everyone has good days and bad days, and self-esteem can go up and down. If you're feeling low and unhappy about yourself, remind yourself ...
- You're as important as anyone else.
- It's OK to make mistakes.
- You deserve to be treated kindly.
- You don't have to be perfect, or good at everything.
- It's fine to be yourself.

MENTAL ILLNESS

Sometimes, though, bad feelings, worries or fears can be so overwhelming, they can actually make you ill. This is known as mental illness, and it's just as real as any other kind of illness.

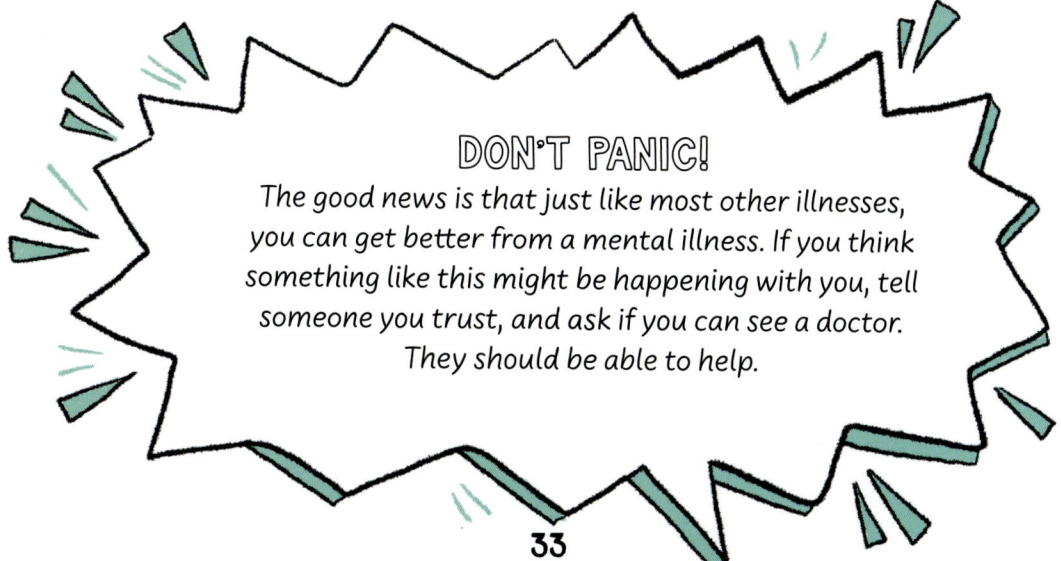

Mental illness can take the form of ...
- **depression**, where you feel sad, numb or unable to do anything.
- **anxiety**, where you worry or panic so much that it takes over your life.
- **OCD**, or **Obsessive-Compulsive Disorder**, where you can't stop thinking about or doing something, such as washing your hands.
- **phobias**, where you're terrified of something, even if it's harmless.

DON'T PANIC!
The good news is that just like most other illnesses, you can get better from a mental illness. If you think something like this might be happening with you, tell someone you trust, and ask if you can see a doctor. They should be able to help.

STRANGE NEW FEELINGS

Feeling moody or stressed can be hard, but at least you've felt those things before. As you go through puberty, you might start to feel new, different kinds of feelings, too.

HAVING A CRUSH
A crush is when you have a strong feeling of being attracted to someone, or 'fancying' them. It might even feel like you love them – even if you don't really know them!

It could be someone in your class, a neighbour or a friend ...
Or maybe an older sibling's friend ...
It could be a famous actor or pop star ...
Or even a teacher! EMBARRASSING!

HOW IT FEELS
A crush can feel really powerful, even unbearable. You might wish you could be with that person, or even kiss them ... but you can also feel REALLY embarrassed, and not want them to find out! Seeing them can make you blush, or feel awkward and shy.

BOYFRIENDS AND GIRLFRIENDS
As you get older, people you know might start having boyfriends and girlfriends whom they kiss and cuddle. You might too. But remember, you don't have to do this if you don't want to – even if someone else wants you to. You can always say no.

NEW FEELINGS
As you get older, it's normal to start having sexual feelings about people you like. It's also normal to touch your genitals. This is called masturbation, and most people do it! But it's private. No one should do this to you, or ask you to do it to them. If that happens, tell a trusted adult straightaway.

FRIENDS AND FITTING IN

During puberty, friends can become a bigger part of your life. A lot of girls worry about making friends, fitting in and what other people think.

Having friends and a social life can be great!
- People to talk to about your parents, your feelings or the changes of puberty.
- Sharing hobbies and fun activities.
- Having a gang to hang out with at school.

But sometimes, social life can be stressful too. You might find yourself ...
- Worrying that you're weird, or that people don't like you.
- Wanting to fit in and be 'popular'.
- Or maybe wanting to NOT fit in, and be different!
- Falling out with friends, or changing friendship groups.

When friendships go wrong, it can be REALLY upsetting. It's even worse if you're being left out on purpose, or bullied.

WHAT CAN YOU DO?
If you're upset, you could talk to a parent or relative. Pets can be very comforting too, as they don't judge you!

Check out the de-stressing and self-esteem tips on pages 31 and 32 – they might help. And if you're being bullied, you should always tell a trusted adult.

I'M READING!

DON'T PANIC!
What if you just don't fit in, and find it hard to make friends? Or you're shy, or can't seem to find the right things to say? There are actually loads of people who feel like this. You could try hobbies or clubs where you might find people more like you.

And remember, as you get older you'll meet a wider range of people, and get to choose whom you hang out with. And it's also fine if you prefer your own company. Lots of people are like that, too!

SAY NO TO SEXISM!

Has anyone ever told you something you want to do, wear or try out is for boys and not girls? Or made you feel you should be kind and look after other people, but not expected boys to do the same? That's sexism!

LOOK OUT FOR IT!
There ARE some differences between girls and boys. But some people think that girls and boys should stick to particular hairstyles, school subjects, jobs, ways of behaving or even colours for their clothes! You might think that sounds silly – and it is.

But sexism like this is all around us, in adverts, books, movies and in the way many people talk. It can sometimes affect you without you even realising.

GIRLS CAN!

So if there's something you want to do, but feel you 'shouldn't' because you're a girl, stop and think. You can be any kind of girl you want. Don't be held back by what anyone thinks girls 'should' be like.

JUST BE YOU

Maybe you love make-up, sew your own dresses and have long hair. But you also want to learn the drums, fly planes or be a robot scientist. Well, you can. You don't have to fit into any kind of box.

That goes for other life choices, too. You don't have to get married or have children, for example. It's your choice.

BOYS GET IT TOO!

Boy can also be made to feel they shouldn't do 'girly' things, thanks to sexism. It's nonsense. They can do anything they want, just like girls!

WHEN DOES IT END?

How long is all this going to go on?!

Well, it normally takes a few years to get through all the changes of puberty – from around age 10 or 11 on average, to around 14 or 15.

That might seem like a VERY long time. But it's probably better for it to happen bit by bit, instead of waking up one day to find you've grown up overnight!

ER ... WHO ARE YOU?

And remember, you don't spend every moment dealing with puberty, or thinking about it. You're still busy doing other stuff, learning, having fun and living your life!

HERE TO STAY

The point of puberty is to make you grow up, so the changes it brings are mostly permanent, like your new body shape, body hair and adult height.

HOW LONG DO PERIODS LAST?
As for periods, they usually go on until the age of about 50, when they finally stop. If you get pregnant, they also stop until after the baby is born.

SWEET 16!
But going through puberty itself, and all the changes and emotions that come with it, is mostly over by the age of 16.

WHAT HAPPENS THEN?
As puberty slows down and stops, you'll get used to all those changes that might have once seemed scary or confusing. You'll probably start to feel calmer, more confident and less moody – if you've been having problems with any of these! Spots and period pain usually get better, too.

And soon you'll be ready for the next stage of your life, and all the adventures to come!

PUBERTY TIMELINE

Here's a handy at-a-glance guide to when the big changes of puberty are most likely to happen, from the first body changes to the final growth spurts!

AGE	7	8	9	10	11
BREASTS	← Start growing around 8 to 11 →				
BODY HAIR			← Starts growing around 9 or 10 →		
BODY SHAPE			← Starts changing around 9 or 10 →		
SPOTS	← Can appear at any time during puberty →				
HEIGHT	You're already growing when puberty starts!				
PERIODS			← Start somewhere between 9 and 13 →		

DON'T PANIC!

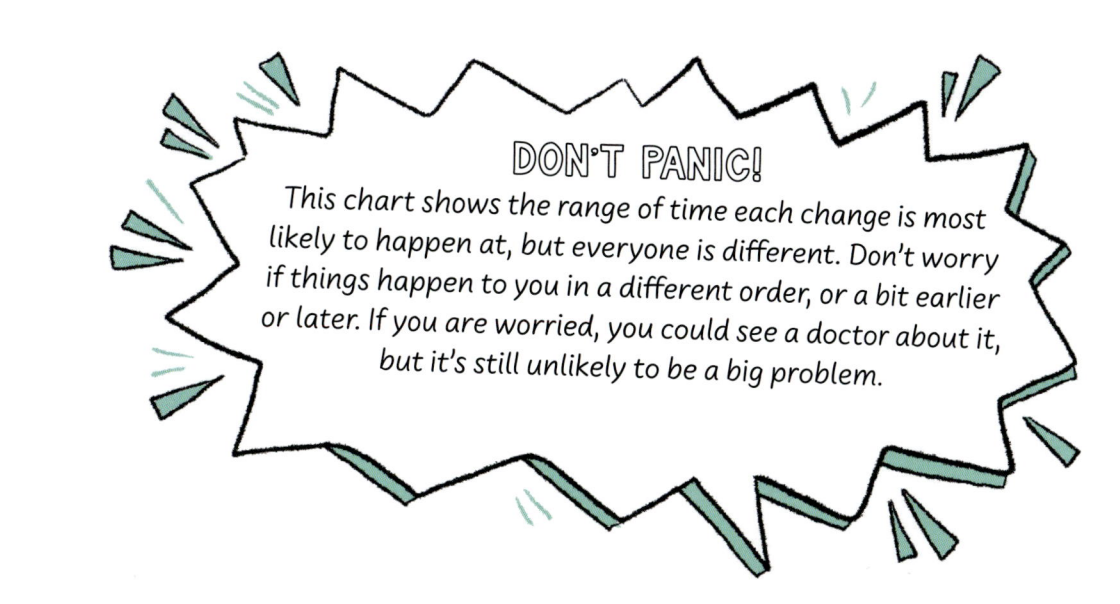

This chart shows the range of time each change is most likely to happen at, but everyone is different. Don't worry if things happen to you in a different order, or a bit earlier or later. If you are worried, you could see a doctor about it, but it's still unlikely to be a big problem.

| 12 | 13 | 14 | 15 | 16 | 17 |

← Finish growing around 16 or 17 →

← Fully grown around 13 or 14 →

← Fully changed around 14 or 15 →

← Some people might get spots after puberty, but they usually become less severe →

← Adult height by around 14 to 16 →

→ Carry on until around 50! →

FREQUENTLY ASKED QUESTIONS

More questions? Maybe you'll find one of them here ...

WHY DO I HAVE TO GROW UP?
Good question! As humans, we go through a life cycle, and we have to go through puberty to be able to have our own children. But even if you don't want children, the changes of puberty help your brain to grow up too, and make your body bigger and stronger. That means you can have your own home, have a job, travel the world, and do all kinds of other things that children can't do. If people didn't grow up and spend most of their lives as adults, there would be way too many children, and not enough adults to look after them!

WHY AM I SO HUNGRY?
During puberty, you're growing a lot. As well as growing taller, your body shape changes, your reproductive system grows and changes in your brain use up a lot of energy, too. So you need plenty of food! Try to eat fresh, healthy food most of the time, and eat as many different types of food as you can to give your body all the nutrients it needs.

ARE MY BREASTS TOO SMALL OR TOO BIG?
Breasts come in a huge range of shapes and sizes, which are all normal – from almost flat to bigger than your head! However, all breasts – no matter what size – can make milk to feed a baby.

WHAT IF I GET MY PERIOD AND I DON'T HAVE ANY PADS?

Period emergency! This is why it's a good idea to carry a little period pack around with you - but it can still happen (and HAS happened to most women!). Go to a toilet as soon as you can, and wrap a long piece of toilet paper around the middle part of your pants lots of times to make an emergency pad that will work for a while.

Then, if possible, ask another girl or woman - a friend, a nice teacher, or whoever you can find! - if they have a spare pad you could have. Most women know how it feels, and will be happy to help. Remember, some schools, libraries, health centres and even shops have free sanitary products, and some toilets have them in vending machines.

SHOULD I KEEP A FRIEND'S SECRET?

Usually, if a friend tells you a secret - like who they have a crush on - yes, you should keep it. Friends should be able to trust you not to gossip about them, and it's good to know you can talk to a friend without them telling the world what you've said!

However, there are times when it is a good idea to share the secret with a grown-up whom you trust - for example, if a friend tells you they are being abused or hurt by someone. In that case, you could talk it over with an adult you trust, like a parent, relative or sympathetic teacher.

GLOSSARY

Adrenal glands Glands in your body that release the hormone adrenaline.
Adrenaline A hormone that makes your heart beat faster so you can move quickly if needed.
Anus The hole where poo comes out of your body.
Anxiety A feeling of fear, worry or panic.
Areola The circular area of skin around the nipple, which is often darker than your other skin.
Breast bud A small bump that forms under the nipple as a breast starts to grow.
Cervix The opening of the womb, or uterus.
Clitoris A sensitive bump found near the front of the vulva.
Crush A powerful feeling of being attracted to someone.
Depression A mental illness that can make you feel sad, numb or empty.
Egg cell A type of female cell released from the ovaries, that can join with a male sperm cell to become a baby.
Fallopian tubes Tubes that carry egg cells from the ovaries to the womb or uterus.
Genitals A name for the sex organs, such as the vulva and vagina.
Hormones Chemical signals released by glands around the body, which control the way some body parts work or grow.
Hypothalamus A brain part that releases some types of hormone.
Immune system A body system that keeps out or kills harmful germs.
Insulin A hormone that helps your body use glucose (or sugar) for energy.
Labia The folds of skin around the vagina.
Life cycle The changes that a living thing goes through during its life, such as being born, growing up and reproducing.
Menstrual cycle A series of changes that a woman's or older girl's body goes through roughly once a month, including the ovaries releasing an egg, and having a period.
Mental illness An illness that affects your mood, emotions or behaviour.
OCD (Obsessive-Compulsive Disorder) A mental illness that makes you have repeated thoughts, worries or behaviour.
Ovaries Two organs in the female body that release both hormones and egg cells.
Pancreas A large gland behind the stomach that releases insulin.
Period The part of the menstrual cycle when blood comes out of the vagina, usually for a few days.
Phobia A mental illness or disorder that makes you feel an extreme fear of something.

Pituitary gland A gland in the brain that releases several hormones, and also controls various other hormone glands.
Pubic hair Hair that starts to grow around and above the genitals as you go through puberty.
Reproductive system A body system used to reproduce, or make and give birth to babies.
Sebum An oily substance released from the skin, which can contribute to spots and oily hair.
Self-esteem A feeling of self-acceptance and being happy with yourself and who you are.
Sexism Prejudice or stereotyped expectations about people based on whether they are male or female.
Sperm cell A type of male cell that can join with a female egg cell to become a baby.
Urethra A tube connected to your bladder that urine, or wee, comes out of.
Uterus Another name for the womb.
Vagina A tube of muscle linking the womb to the vulva.
Vulva The outer parts of the female genitals, including the labia, clitoris and opening to the vagina.
Womb An organ in the female body where babies can grow, and where period blood comes from.

BOOKS

My Period: Find your flow and feel proud of your period!
By Milli Hill
Wren & Rook, 2021

Be Happy Be You: The teenage guide to boost happiness and resilience
By Becky Goddard-Hill and Penny Alexander
Collins, 2020

My Body's Changing: A Girl's Guide to Growing Up
By Anita Ganeri
Franklin Watts, 2020

Ruby Luna's Moontime
By Tessa Venuti Sanderson
Castenetto & Co, 2020

INDEX

acne 20
adrenaline 10-11
anus 9
anxiety 25, 33
areolae *(one: areola)* 14
armpits 7, 22

babies 6, 8-9, 14, 16-17, 44
blood 16-19
boobs 7, 14-15, 42-44
boyfriends 35
brain 4, 11, 25-26, 28-29, 44
bras 15
breast buds 14
breasts *see boobs*
bullying 36-37

caffeine 27
cervix 8
clitoris 9
crushes 34-35
cycle (menstrual) 16-17, 19

depression 33

egg cells 8, 17
emotions *(see also feelings)* 11, 30-31, 41
exercise 25, 27, 31

fallopian tubes 8, 17
feelings *(see also emotions)* 4-5, 25, 30-36
food 10, 24-25, 44
friendships 36, 45

genitals *(see also vulva, penis)* 9
girlfriends 35

glands 11
  adrenal glands 11
  hypothalamus 11
  pancreas 11
  pituitary glands 11
growth spurts 7, 12-13, 42

hair *(see also pubic hair)* 7, 20, 22-23, 25, 40, 42-43
hair removal 23
height (body) 4, 12-13, 40, 42-43
hormones 10-11, 20, 30

insulin 10-11

labia 9
life cycles 6, 44
love 34-35

masturbation 35
mental illnesses 33
mood swings 11, 30, 32

nipples 14

OCD (obsessive-compulsive disorder) 33
oestrogen 11
ovaries 8, 11, 17

penis 17
period pants 18
period products 18-19, 45
periods 4, 9, 16-19, 30, 41-43, 45
phobias 33
pregnancy 6, 8
progesterone 11
pubic hair 7, 22

reproductive system 8, 44

sanitary pads 18, 45
sanitary products *(see period products)*
self-esteem 32, 37
sex 17, 29
sexism 38-39
skin 7, 20-21, 23, 25
sleep 26-27
sperm cells 17
spots 7, 20-21, 42-43
stress 25, 30, 32, 34
stretch marks 21
sweat 7, 20, 23

tampons 19

urethra 9
uterus *(see womb)*

vagina 8-9, 16-17, 19
vulva 9, 22

womb 8, 17, 19
  lining 17